WHEN
Heaven
MEETS
Earth

CARL WAYNE WHITECOTTON

WESTBOW
PRESS®
A DIVISION OF THOMAS NELSON
& ZONDERVAN

WestBow Press books may be ordered through booksellers or by contacting:

WestBow Press
A Division of Thomas Nelson & Zondervan
1663 Liberty Drive
Bloomington, IN 47403
www.westbowpress.com
844-714-3454

ISBN: 978-1-6642-4317-0 (sc)
ISBN: 978-1-6642-4318-7 (e)

Library of Congress Control Number: 2021917151

Print information available on the last page.

WestBow Press rev. date: 09/16/2021

Contents

Contents

The Card-Punching Christian

I believed that I was a strong Christian. I had an amazing wife and four awesome children. We were saved and baptized, went to church most Sundays, and got our cards punched as members who, yes, were there.

We could slip in and out of church without too many people noticing that we were there. We never got involved in events, dinners, Bible studies, or other activities, and we avoided talking to anyone other than to say good morning to the door greeter if he spoke first. I was happy with our church attendance and believed God expected nothing more of us.

Then on a November day four and a half years ago, I got sick. It changed my life and my family members' lives forever.

In writing this book, I hope to encourage you to seek a friendship with God, Jesus, and the Holy Spirit, and to get the fire inside you raging for more Jesus. No matter what you do, you can never have enough Jesus. This is my testimony.

I am just your average guy. I worked a union factory job and used weekends to catch up on work around the house and yard. I worked as much overtime as I could just to stash money away for the unexpected events in life that we all face at the worst moments. It was a chilly November evening, and we were cooking over a bonfire and just chatting about the kids and life in general. I had worked eighty-four hours that week and was really drained of energy. I noticed my wife looking at me with concern. She called me to the side and asked if I was feeling OK. She told me my left eye was drooping and that I looked like I'd had a stroke. I told her not to worry; I was just tired and would be fine tomorrow.

I continued to go to work without having a doctor check it out, and each day there was a pain in my left eye that got worse. I put eye drops in my eye to keep the severe pain from preventing me from working and was using about a bottle of painkiller each week. My eye started to swell shut. It turned pink and then red, and it felt like it was going to pop out of my head.

My wife said I should go and have a doctor look at it as there was something severely wrong. I told her it was just pink eye, and I would go to the doctor in the spring, when overtime ended, and have it checked out. I continued to work twelve-hour days with one eye. My boss told me, "There is going to come a point in time when, for your safety, I'm going to have to send you home. So you better think about getting medical attention."

My wife was telling me every day that I needed to go see a doctor. So I finally agreed. I said, "Well, there's something wrong with my eye—pink eye or something. So I'll see an eye doctor."

She agreed. She said, "At least I can get you to see a doctor of some sort."

We went to the eye doctor, and he said, "I don't know what this is." He pulled out books. You know you're in trouble when a doctor pulls out books. Finally he said, "I'd like to send you to a eye specialist."

I went to see the specialist. When we got to the doctor's office, he used the strange telescope-looking device with a light on it. He told me I had holes in my left eye. In order to know the extent of whatever was going on, I would need to have an MRI. After he got the results from the MRI, he would call us and let us know what they found.

2

Meeting Jesus

For the MRI, the specialist sent me to a hospital with a brand-new MRI machine there. The drive to the hospital seemed to take forever.

While sitting in the waiting room, a man came out and introduced himself to my wife and me. He told us that he normally dealt with nuclear medicine, but since he had no patients of his own, he was going to sit in and observe.

The technician for the MRI and the nuclear technician walked me back to the MRI machine. As they helped me lie down in the correct position, all covered up, the phone rang in the tech booth. The MRI technician was called away to another problem and asked the nuclear technician to take over. The nuclear technician informed me that I was in good hands because he used to run the MRI machine. He left the room, telling me not to move as he prepared the machine.

Normally an MRI machine has red lights, but this one had a blue one. I remember being fascinated by this blue light. As I looked at the blue light, something began to happen. I could see through it. *That's weird,* I thought. I looked up through this blue light and saw heaven. I then ascended into heaven.

That was the first time I saw Jesus!

I want you to know nothing like that had ever happened any other time in my life. It's so important that I stress this.

Jesus said something to me that no one would've ever known, except Jesus. He said, "Carl, I know you're scared, but you won't admit it." He had my attention right there.

Now think about that. I was taught never to show fear. He went right behind this mask of bravery that I had perfected and said exactly what I was feeling.

Then he went one step further and said, "I will be with you through all of this." At the time I didn't know what "all of this" was. I still don't know what "all of this" is going to be.

Jesus said, "I will be with you through all of this, and every time you get scared, I will hold your right hand."

The only thing I could think to say to him was, "I love you."

Let's fast-forward just a second here to the present day, four and a half years later. If I get scared, nervous, or excited, Jesus holds my hand, and it's amazing. Just totally amazing.

As soon as I spoke to Jesus, I descended back into the MRI.

When the MRI was finished, the nuclear technician

came back into the room to help me up from the MRI machine. He let me know that they would send everything to the specialist.

Knowing the technician had seen the MRI pictures, I decided to ask his opinion about what doctor's note I should turn in to work. I had a note from the eye doctor writing me off work for three days. I also had a note from the specialist writing me off from work indefinitely.

His response was, "Which one did you get first? Which one did you get last? What do you think Jesus would do? Look, man, if they have to take your eye, don't you think God would give you a job for a one-eyed man?"

I went out to the lobby where my wife was waiting for me. After telling her what I saw and how I'd met Jesus, she said, "What was 'all of this'? Why didn't you ask questions?"

My goodness. I'd been in front of Jesus, and I couldn't think of anything to ask. It was beautiful. The peace, goodness, and love from Jesus was so overpowering I could hardly speak. It took everything I had just to say, "I love you." I'm telling you, it was indescribably beautiful.

As we were discussing meeting Jesus and my conversation with the tech, we stopped at work to turn in my doctor's note, writing me off work indefinitely. God blessed me with FMLA.

We went home and waited for the specialist to give us a call.

That evening, the specialist called and said, "You've got to get to a big hospital immediately."

I asked, "Why?"

He said, "There are things going on, and you're just going to have to have brain surgery. There is a lesion that goes through your eye into your brain. And I don't want to use the C-word, but it could be cancer."

I said, "Well, I can't go tomorrow because I have to go to church."

He replied, "No. You need to leave now."

I said, "Well I can't go immediately. I have to go to church first."

He gave me a choice of two hospitals. We chose the hospital closest to where we had family, though it was still a five-hour drive from us. But we knew we could get help with our kids and whatever the situation would be.

Shortly after speaking with the doctor, I decided to call a man from our church whom I had spoken to many times away from church about Jesus. He was not available, but his wife asked if she could help.

I told her about my eye and what the doctor said. I then told her what I had seen during the MRI and what Jesus had told me.

She suddenly got very excited. I could tell she was jumping up and down as she said, "You're going to live! Don't you understand what he was saying?"

3

The Prayer

Our church was performing a play for Christmas the next day. We decided to go to the play and calm our nerves after the news we received from the doctor. This was on Saturday evening. We enjoyed the amazing performance by our church. I believe it was about Christmas throughout time. After the play, we were standing in the lobby, getting ready to walk out the doors and head home, when the man I had tried calling the night before walked up to me and said, "Pastor Rick would like to pray for you before you leave tonight." Pastor Rick prayed for my healing that night. He also told me that I needed to be prayed for at the altar in church the next day. My wife and I discussed it and decided I needed to be prayed for at the altar before we headed out on a five-hour road trip.

At the end of service the next day, the Pastor Rick called me and my wife up to the altar. He explained my situation to the flock and proceeded to tell everyone that my wife and I needed the whole church to stand in the gap and pray along with him for my healing.

I have never stood in front of so many people as I did that day, with all their attention on me. I could feel their eyes all on me. Pastor Rick laid his hand on top of my head and started praying. I didn't hear a word he said. All I could see was a brilliant light, the most beautiful white light you could ever imagine. It was so pure and bright. And what I felt flooding over my body was an indescribable feeling of love. The next thing I knew, I was on my back on the floor and couldn't move a muscle. Tears were running down my cheeks.

I don't know how long I lay on the floor. In asking my wife later, she had no idea of the time either. I feel that it is necessary to tell you that I had seen people slain in the spirit on TV and never believed it was real. I always thought it was a show on TV for the money, that the people who did get slain were faking it. Boy did I get corrected that day in church. God, Jesus, and the Holy Spirit showed up for me that day and flooded me with their love.

It was snowing as we were driving home from church. We normally don't get snow where we live. If we do, it's normally melted by the next morning. But even though my wife said she didn't have a worry in the world after having been prayed for—she didn't worry about me, the snow, the drive, or anything that was occurring in our lives at the time; she was definitely high on Jesus—we decided to wait until the next morning to head for the hospital.

That evening my eye swelled even more. My wife said she thought it was going to pop since it had gotten so large. She kept telling me, "God is working on it."

4

Jesus in the Ambulance

The next day happened to be my birthday, December 5. We entered the hospital through the emergency room. After being admitted and assigned a room, they told me they also needed to do an MRI. After the MRI, I was told I needed brain surgery. The brain surgeon who was waiting to do the surgery told me, "You have some kind of major brain infection going on." He said he would take a bone saw and cut the cap off of my head, lift it off to one side. He would use a suction device and go down in between each crevice of the brain. He said, "The operation takes about eight hours. And by the way, chances are you're not going to live through it. You probably won't make it. Tell your wife and kids goodbye."

What a helpless situation. This is when you really, *really* feel helpless. I wondered, *Do I let him do it? Do I just say, "Forget it"? What am I going to do?* So I decided to let him do it. My wife told me I was too stubborn to leave earth this way anyhow.

The surgeon planned the surgery for six o'clock that evening. When it came time for the surgery, an intern came to my room. This intern said, "Unfortunately we do not have the right equipment to perform this surgery. We've got an ambulance ready to take you to a teaching hospital. They are going to have a surgical team on standby, waiting for your arrival. You'll be pulling out of here in just a few minutes. So say goodbye to your family. Say goodbye to your kids."

I've never had to do anything like that before, and I don't ever want to do it again. I want you to know that it was the hardest thing I ever had to do, to hug each kid, tell them I love them, and tell them goodbye. I had to look each of them in the eye and promise to fight with everything I've got to come back to them. Their cries just ripped my heart out.

After all the crying and goodbyes, the ambulance crew was there to take me to the teaching hospital. They refused to let my wife ride with us. One problem right after another. They said forms hadn't been filled out that allowed her to ride along. So my wife had to call her mother, and she took my wife.

I was okay with the ambulance ride until we got right outside the hospital. It was snowing, and the roads were a little icy. The ambulance fishtailed. I thought, *Oh no! I'm gonna get killed in an ambulance wreck.* And that's when I got scared.

Let's go back to the promise that Jesus made: "Every time you get scared, I'll hold your right hand." He made good on his promise. Jesus came through the wall of that ambulance. He didn't say a word; he just held my hand.

I was so afraid because I thought he was going to take me. I wasn't ready to go, and I'm not ready to go now. I'm ready to fight the good fight and bring many to Jesus. That's what I do.

While this was going on, I could hear the ambulance drivers talking to each other. We arrived at the hospital just minutes after Jesus left the ambulance. The EMTs covered me with a warm blanket. One of them said, "We hope you're warm enough. After all, it is winter."

When they opened the doors, I saw that we couldn't get close because there were so many ambulances. My guess is that we were over a half a block away. It was rough getting across the parking lot because of the snow that had melted and refrozen into ice with tire marks in it. I felt like I was in some kind of a giant shake machine.

Even though they sent my MRI with me from the last hospital, the surgeon wanted his own MRI. So the first thing they did was send me for another MRI. While I was getting the new MRI, reality set in, and my mind was racing about a hundred miles per hour.

When I got back to my room, my wife and mother-in-law were there. We started talking about the events that led us to the teaching hospital. I knew my wife was concerned that they sent me to a teaching hospital. She kept asking, "How is a teaching hospital better than a regular hospital?" Keep in mind that we looked at this as a personal matter and didn't tell anyone outside of my wife's family and our kids.

I want you to know how much of a blessing my mother-in-law is. Out of nowhere she gets a phone call from her daughter, who is crying, drives her almost two hundred miles, and waits to see what the brain surgeon has to say. Then she drove home, so she could work in the morning.

We were still in disbelief about everything because we just didn't know what was going to happen at this point. Then when the brain surgeon comes in, you know it's always going to be bad news. Or at least that's how I felt.

I didn't realize that Jesus had another plan.

This doctor was mad. I thought, *Oh, boy, this is going to be bad.*"

He asked, "What happened on that ambulance ride?"

"I don't know what you are talking about."

"Oh, yes you do. What happened on that ambulance ride?"

"Sorry, Doc, I really don't know what you're talking about." He had about four or five other questions. Finally I had to say, "Well, maybe you should tell me."

Then he says, "This infection that was in your brain, that was killing you, is no longer in your brain. There is a perfect wall protecting your brain."

The whole room was shocked. My wife and I just sat

there with no response. When I was in the ambulance I was not going to live through the night. And now the infection was no longer in my brain?

Thank God my mother-in-law, Kathy, was there because we didn't even know what to say at this point. I'll remember what she said forever. Now it didn't sound right, but in a way it does.

She said, "You mean he's not dying? Wait a minute, something isn't right here. This has been an emotional roller-coaster, and he's in no danger right now?" Thank God she was there because she asked the questions we were too shocked to ask.

Then the doctor said, "In the morning we will go in for surgery, but we're going to do it differently than what you would expect."

Uh oh. What weird thing are they going to do to me here? I wondered. I was getting nervous again.

"We are going to take a little robot and stick him in your nose. He's going to crawl up your nose and behind your eye. Then he'll go up and around your brain. The robot is going to take samples every step of the way."

"Interesting." That's all I could say.

The doctor continued, "We want to know what's going on and how it just changed. What's going on with your brain? So we are going to explore. We're just trying to make sure that you are okay."

Before surgery, my wife and I were talking, and I got

scared. And the next thing you know, Jesus was there again, holding my hand. This time it was different because my wife was holding my hand, too, so she also felt Jesus. How wonderful, how beautiful. Through my illness, she got to feel Jesus for the first time in her life. So you know this illness is all about miracles. It's all about God. It's all about Jesus. It's all about the Holy Spirit and what they can do.

Like I said at the beginning of all this, I was a pew-sitter, and I never saw anything. Now I can't imagine a day without my Father being in my life. I just don't know what I would do.

So I went into surgery. The robot went around my brain and took samples and whatever else it was programmed to do. They wanted to keep me in the hospital for a couple days. I don't remember exactly how long they kept me in the hospital. Since Jesus held my hand, it was one long day for me. I lost track of and didn't care about time. All I cared about—and all I continue to care about—is serving my Father, and I want to be a good follower of Jesus. This is important to me. I'm not perfect; I'll never be perfect. I'm not even worthy of following Jesus. But I need him. I need Jesus in my life, and you do too. And as you get into this book, you're going to understand how much you need Jesus to step into your life.

Before I left the teaching hospital, God gave me a message to give to the world. He said, "I have more love to give than you can imagine. All you have to do is ask."

The first time I delivered that message was in front of a crowd of three hundred people, and I was scared to death! I was totally shocked when the crowd stood up and cheered on God.

Later I was caught delivering God's message anywhere there were people, including the post office, food pantry, and parking lots.

5

After the Operation

N ow the operation is over with, I don't know why they called it an operation. It makes no sense to me. It's just a robot going around and collecting samples in your brain. So it was done and over with, and I recovered and survived. Little did I know life as I knew it was over. I have a new life, and it's a beautiful life.

That afternoon I couldn't rest at all. There I was, walking the hallways. The nurses said, "You can't walk. You just had brain surgery!"

But I walked. I walked a lot; I wore out the staff. They let my wife walk with me, and I wore out my wife. The nurses called the doctor, and he said, "Let him go. Let him walk anywhere he wants to go. That's a good sign because he won't get blood clots inside his legs. Let him walk if that's what he wants to do."

The first strange thing happened while walking the hallways. There was a woman, and I assumed the results for her loved one were not good. She was crying hysterically; it was horrible. I couldn't stand it. It broke my heart. I asked aloud, "Father, isn't there anything you can do to put some peace in her?"

The next thing I knew, in the middle of a big scream, she stopped, walked over, and sat down. She was in absolute peace. I stopped walking long enough to ask what happened. I was very, very nervous. Shocked you might say. What in the world was going on? Nothing like that had ever happened to me.

I was released from the hospital after a couple days. We went back to my wife's family, gathered our children, and drove the five hours home.

Shortly after we arrived home, the phone rang. It was the surgeon. "I have some bad news, and it will be necessary for you to return. Somewhere in your head there is cancer. I'm not sure that I believe this because it is not on the MRI. The doctor in pathology says that it is in one of the samples the robot took. We are going to have to do another surgery, and you will be kept under until we find the cancer."

So we went back early to visit with my wife's family for a couple days. Her family members are true warriors. I love those people; they came through for us. After the visit, we drove the two hundred miles to the teaching hospital yet again.

I went in for the surgery the next day.

The robot was so smart it forgot to label the samples

during the first surgery. During the second surgery, they found the cancer on my left cheekbone. While I was under, the doctor cut out over a half-inch of the cheekbone.

When I woke up, I looked in the mirror because I knew it didn't feel right. My cheek was sunk in. It was hideous, gross to look at.

We spent the night at my in-laws' house. I prayed for God to use me. The next morning, the Holy Spirit came to me and said, "I want you to go over to the apartment complex where your sister lives. I have three people I need you to pray for. The first one is Jane, the second one is Tom, and you'll know the third one when you meet them." I was scared. You need to remember that at this time, I hadn't prayed for anyone else.

I called my sister. "Do you know Jane?"

"Yes I do."

"Do you know Tom?"

"Yes I do."

I said, "Okay, I'll be right there." When we arrived I told my sister, "I need you to take me to see Jane."

She replied, "Oh, you can't go and talk about God like you do. She'll run you off."

"Don't put God in a box," I told her. "If God's sending me, he has a reason. What, I don't know." So we went to Jane's house.

When Jane invited us in, I told her, "I'm here to pray for you." You don't know how nervous I was.

She asked, "What for?"

I tried to say, "God's going to heal you," but the words wouldn't come out. Instead, a word I had never used before came out. "I'm here to soothe you."

She looked at me and smiled. "Just soothe away."

As I was praying, I noticed a few things. Jane was sitting in a chair and wearing an oxygen mask. I also noticed a hole in the back of her heel, and the bone showing. It looked terrible. But as I started to pray for Jane, I felt the Holy Spirit come through my arms and into my hands. I felt him go into her body.

"What is that? My body's starting to tremble," she responded.

She was so curious. I told her, "That's the Holy Spirit. Just let him do what he's going to do."

She replied, "Okay."

I didn't think I did too badly as a first-time prayer warrior. So I kind of rushed it as quickly as I could.

I got through it, and she just sat there, shaking and trembling. I had no clue what this was developing into. When we got ready to leave, Jane's personal aide came in from one of the other rooms. My body started shaking, and when she made eye contact with me, she started shaking.

I'm thankful my wife's always right beside me because she said, "That has to be the third person. Look at how both your bodies are responding. You're both shaking, and you haven't said a word to each other."

I walked up to her and said, "I'm supposed to pray for you."

She said, "Go ahead."

"I'm going to have to lay hands on you." I thought, *That is a weird thing to say.* Again she told me to go ahead. So I put my hand on her head and started praying. I felt the Holy Spirit going into her body, just like I did with Jane.

"What is that?" she asked. She seemed kind of scared.

I told her, "Relax. It's just the Holy Spirit, and he's here to help, whatever your problem is."

She never told me what her problem was. While I was praying, the Holy Spirit whispered in my ear, "She is pregnant." I turned and shared with my wife.

The aide started shaking badly. It was time for her to get off work. After prayer she said, "There's no way I can drive." So she laid down on the couch.

It was awesome. I had no clue what took place, but I knew something did because the Holy Spirit is not going to order you in and have you pray for someone and nothing happen.

We left Jane's home and I asked my sister, "Can you take me over to Tom's house?" She agreed, so we walked in a zigzag pattern around the apartment complex to Tom's house.

Tom was in a different situation; he was in a wheelchair. As soon as he opened the door, I could feel the darkness.

He was in a really dark place. I told him, "Tom, I'm here to pray for you."

He said, "You can pray all you want, but nothing is going to happen."

I thought about it for a minute. I was still new to all this, so I said, "Okay. Just so I can be obedient, I'm still going to pray for you."

I looked around the room for any signs that would give me a clue to help because he wasn't offering anything other than the fact that it wasn't going to work. The only thing I saw was about a hundred pills loose on the table. I'm sure most of you have been in situations where what others are going through is really dark.

I said, "Okay, let's pray." I prayed, and again I felt the Holy Spirit. I wasn't really sure what happened.

When I finished praying, he said, "Thank you, but nothing happened."

"Well I'm not too sure. I'll check up on you in a few days, and we'll see what happens."

After we left Tom's house, I gathered my family, and we went home.

I did a whole lot of praying once we got home. I still didn't understand what God was doing. I may be naive. I still don't know what God's doing, but I know that I'm in a place where I need to be. I need to be closer to Jesus all the time.

A couple days passed, and we decided to check on

people. We wanted to know if anything happened. I was so curious.

I got in touch with Jane first. She was so thankful, but I didn't know what she was thanking me for. So I started asking questions. I wanted to know what was going on.

She asked, "Remember the hole that went down to my bone on the back of my heel?"

"Yes, I remember." The doctors had been trying for four years to get that hole to close, and they couldn't. I prayed for her on a Saturday; on Monday they were supposed to amputate her foot. When she went in on Monday, the hole was completely closed, and she got to keep her foot. I thought, *Oh, my Father, What's happened? This is just wild. This is exciting!* I didn't know how to react. Then I asked, "What happened to your personal care worker?"

She answered, "Let me make a couple phone calls, and I'll let you know."

A little later Jane called back. She had gotten all the details on her worker. The reason she was shaking and couldn't walk after prayer was because she had an abortion scheduled for that day. The Holy Spirit came to her and told her, "You have to have this baby. You're not going to kill this baby." She couldn't even get off the couch to drive. When she was finally able to stand, she called and canceled the appointment. She was keeping the baby. Thank you, Jesus.

Then I asked Jane, "Have you heard of anything happening with Tom?" She said she didn't know.

I said, "I got his number. I'll try calling him."

It took a couple days to get hold of Tom. I could tell once I reached him that something changed in his life. "Tom, what happened? Tell me all about it."

He said, "Well you know while you were here I did not feel anything. But my problem was I was giving up. All those pills that you saw lying on that table, I was about to take them until you knocked on the door."

It's so much like our Father in his perfect timing.

Then he continued, "It's so weird because I was still denying everything all the way up until after you left. I didn't feel the Holy Spirit. I didn't see anything. As soon as you shut the door, the Holy Spirit hit me. I was getting ready to commit suicide, and the Holy Spirit said 'Stop feeling sorry for yourself. You are now a preacher.'

"I told him, 'Look at me. I'm all crippled up in this wheelchair,' and he said, 'Go right across the street. There is a nursing home where you can preach.'"

I believe Tom now spends more time across the street as a preacher than he does at home. When you get that visit, when you get those instructions, it's so beautiful to see what God can do through you. That is beautiful. I loved it.

6

Learning My Gifts

It was night. I got off the phone and started crying. God healed all three of those people's lives. I was confused. "Just what are you going to use me for? I don't know anything about healing. Father, if you're going to use me for healings, then you need to teach me something about it. I'm just a total mess. I'm confused, but I'll do whatever you want. You just have to teach me. That's all I ask."

The next day, Sunday, I went to church with my family, and it was beautiful. I felt the Holy Spirit while I was praising and worshipping. When church was over, we didn't dart out. We stayed in our chairs. I could see a guy whom I'd never met because it was a big church marching toward us from the other side of the room. He was walking like he was on a mission. He introduced himself. He's a good guy.

This guy said, "I'm here, and I have a message for you from the Holy Spirit."

I asked, "What?"

He said, "Tonight in this town about a hundred miles from here, there is going to be a healing service by Randy Clark, and the Holy Spirit says you need to be there."

My wife and I just looked at each other like, "You gotta be kidding me," because that was the answer to the prayer. "Yeah, we'll be there." It's wild because I went, and I watched over seven hundred people get healed.

Amazing that this was Randy Clark. It was totally amazing what God did through him and the power of the Holy Spirit falling on everyone in that building. I know it wasn't Randy; it was the Holy Spirit. But still, his calmness and the authority with which he speaks and how he gets to witness what God's doing healing all those people are beautiful.

Afterward, I had the chance to meet Randy, and he said, "I know you."

I replied, "No, you don't."

I want you to know, he probably did. The Holy Spirit often tells me to go somewhere, and he gives them a visual image of me before I get there. They expect me, and they know who I am. I love that. At first it shocked me. Now I just smile.

Before we had the chance to talk, a guy in a wheelchair came rolling up, and Randy immediately turned his attention to praying for this man. I probably should have waited, but I didn't. Because of the long drive, I went home.

The guy who invited me over there told me the next

Sunday at church, "I got some videos I want you to watch in your spare time." They were videos from an annual global healing conference held in January 2012 from Randy Clark. This was what was really hard to get hold of—what God can do with time.

The next evening, my wife and I started watching one of the videos. Keep in mind that when we were watching the video on our couch, it was 2017.

We were almost through the video when Randy said, "Somebody who is watching this has a problem with their left cheekbone. If that is you, stand up."

I just sat there like a bump on a log. After all, it's a five-year-old video, and I'm at home. The next thing I knew, my wife elbowed me and said, "Get up. He is talking to you."

"I'm not getting up. Not for a five-year-old video in my living room."

She elbowed me again. "Get up! He is talking to you!"

I don't know how she knew he was talking to me, but she was right, he was. So I stood up.

The amazing thing was that on the video, Randy Clark paused until I stood up. Then he said, "Now I want you to say this prayer with me." I said the prayer, and when we got to the end, the video ended. My wife and I decided to go to bed since it was late.

As we got ready to lie down, I was sitting on the end of the bed. My face was tingling. I touched and rubbed my face, and my wife asked, "What's wrong?"

"My face is tingling. It's doing something weird."

She scooted down to the end of the bed, just in time to witness this. My cheekbone grew back completely and perfectly. That was wild. From that moment on, I knew God could do anything. When someone cuts a bone out of you and God grows it back, I'm telling you that's a God that can do anything, and you better get excited. This isn't just a God for me. This is a God for all of us. If he can do this for me, he can do this for you. You have to believe in your heart that he can do anything, and you'll find out that he can.

So the only thing left for me to do was receive treatment for my cancer. Even though the doctor had cut out the bone where it was, they recommended radiation treatment as a follow-up. I had been procrastinating, but I finally decided to get it checked out.

I went to a cancer institute. I'm not going to name names, but their place stunk, and the people were rude. A doctor came in acting like he was the king of the world, and it aggravated me to see him act that way. God told me to treat everyone with God's love. This guy had some horrible behavior, so I fired him.

He told me, "You can't do that!"

I said, "Yes, I can," and then walked out of there.

Humans love to speak curses; for example, "Oh, you're going to die." Stuff like that. Well guess what? You can't make me die. I'm washed in the blood of Jesus. So I found another cancer center in a different state. I liked those people. They were really nice, and it was a clean facility.

First I had to go see the doctor. He naturally got after me about waiting so long. He said, "How could you leave it sitting there for three months? Your body is going to be so riddled with cancer that it isn't funny."

I replied, "Well let's wait and see. I believe it's gone. I believe my Father in heaven took care of everything."

He said, "Okay. I'm going to send you down for a PET scan. When you come back, we can have a meeting and discuss our course of action."

I went down for my PET scan and came back. All he could say was, "Amazing! You have no cancer anywhere in your body. It's gone!"

Thank you, Jesus! All glory to God!

Things really started being different for my family and I as the Holy Spirit continued to give us instructions. One day in morning prayer, the Holy Spirit said to me, "You are going to meet a girl, and her favorite color is green. She is bedridden. She also has cancer, and her initials are A. R."

The search was on. I searched high and low for her with no success. About a month later, I was at work when my wife called me on my break. She said that she met a lady on the internet who inquired about some plants she was selling. The lady thanked her for taking the time to answer her questions. She told my wife, "Because I am sick, most people just dismiss me." What had my wife all excited about this woman was that she signed her message, "A. R."

I immediately told my wife to ask and see if I could call her and pray for her. Next break I called home and was really surprised. My wife said, "You're not going to believe this response. A. R. would love for you to pray for her!"

The next day I called A. R., her favorite color was green, and she had been bedridden for three years. We talked for about thirty minutes, and then I asked her if she believed that Jesus can heal her, and she said yes. I prayed for her and felt the Holy Spirit go down my arm and into the phone. I told her that the Holy Spirit had just gone into the phone, and she should feel him any second. Just like that she was slain in the spirit. I continued to pray for her until she came back to us. She told me that she was twitching, and her body was tingling.

We gave the glory to God. I told her that I would call her later to check on her. I waited about four hours and then called again. When I asked her how she was doing, A. R. was so excited that she said, "I am in the backyard, walking around!"

I said, "Let's give God all the glory." And then we prayed.

After we prayed, I felt there was more to come with her. A week later my wife and I were going into a store. As we opened the door, the Holy Spirit said to me, "Stop and wait. So we waited."

About two minutes later my phone rang, and it was A.

R. I gave my phone to my wife because I was waiting on instructions. I only waited a couple minutes before the Holy Spirit started to speak. He said, "Interrupt them."

I said, "Okay." It was funny because trying to get my wife's attention while she is on the phone is a tough task. She ignored me. I kept saying, "Hun, hun, hun," with no luck.

I finally started tugging at her arm, saying, "Excuse me," and she finally stopped talking and listened.

The Holy Spirit said, "Ask her how many people in her family have died of cancer." I asked, and she started listing family members. And it was many. I soon realized that I was being taught by the Holy Spirit because he already knew.

The Holy Spirit then proceeded to tell me that this was a generational curse and to lift it off this family. So there I was, in the middle of this parking lot, one hand in the air, praying to my Father in heaven to lift this generational curse from them.

It was very emotional and very loud. Thank you, Father, for hearing my prayers and responding to them. I give you all the glory!

The Holy Spirit Sent
Us to Work

One day while praying, the Holy Spirit told me that he was sending us to work at a paint recycling plant almost forty miles away. So I called the temp agency that was placing people there, and they practically hired my wife and I over the phone. Naturally I thought this was interesting. So we went in and were hired to start the next day!

When we started, we were so shocked at what we saw. It seemed like one hundred broken people. There were at least two women who were battered and living in their cars. There were people on drugs and alcohol. There were so many people with sick kids and dying family members.

My wife looked at me and asked, "Where do we start?"

"I don't know," I answered. "Let's just go in and work like we are working for God." So we went in and worked really hard, helping anyone who needed an extra hand. This job was so dirty, and you ruined all your clothes.

Weeks went by, and there was nothing from the Holy Spirit about this job. We still went out almost every night to pray for other people and watched Jesus heal them.

Patience is so hard while you're waiting and seeing so many issues. We also took time to learn everyone's name and what their stories were. We went in every day and was true to Jesus, even though we had to listen to pure filth.

We knew our place was not to judge but to wait and see what God was going to do. When that day arrived, it came without a warning.

I worked on the five-gallon line, which was located next to the one-gallon line. My wife worked on the one-gallon line. She was close enough to hear everything that went on in my line.

First thing, the manager came to me and the only other Christian in the plant and told us to go over a couple of aisles and clean up a two hundred-gallon paint spill. The other guy said, "Good. I know Carl has a story to tell, and I want to hear it."

I smiled and agreed. I told him the same testimony that I'm telling you. We were about halfway through it, and he said, "Don't you see the power in this testimony? Every fork truck is behind this wall of skids, and they are all listening."

I said, "Good. Then I will speak up, so everyone hears."

I continued until the end of my testimony. That's when he said, "I need God's help."

"What do you need?" I asked.

He said, "I need gas."

"How much gas could you possibly need? I saw you drive in this morning."

He said, "I need three gallons to get home!"

At that instant I felt the Holy Spirit in my hands real strong. "God is going to take care of you," I assured him. I was very bold!

We finished cleaning up the paint spill, and it was just a couple of minutes till break. We started toward the one-gallon area, so I could go on break with my wife. What I didn't know was that she was giving my testimony in the one-gallon area.

So as we approached, this guy started running to me, screaming, "Pray for me right here right now!"

This guy's nickname was "Tall" because he towered over everyone. I prayed for Tall. I had no idea why, but it made him very happy!

Then we went to break. My wife and I talked about how powerful the testimony was that day.

When break was over, I went back to the five-gallon area to dump five-gallon buckets of paint. Everyone was shocked at what happened next.

I opened a five-gallon bucket of paint, and it wasn't paint. It was three gallons of gasoline! Everyone was in awe.

The Holy Spirit filled that warehouse immediately! There was no fighting. It was absolute peace. People were so excited that they would walk up and dip their hands in the gas and give their hearts to Jesus. The Holy Spirit stayed there until we all left for the day.

It was a Friday, but no one wanted to leave. People came up to my wife and I and asked if we would come that weekend and pray for their sick family members. All weekend we spent on the road, praying for people. And they were all healed!

My favorite one was a lady whose two kids were sick. The first one I prayed for was a six-year-old girl, who was burning up with a fever of 105 degrees. She was white as a ghost and not moving.

The Holy Spirit said, "Anoint her, and hold her hands and pray." I did exactly as ordered. While I was holding her hands and asking Jesus to heal her, I felt the fever come into my hands and then up to my elbows and out of my elbows. The fever was gone, and she got up and played. Thank you, Jesus!

Next I started talking to her son, who was about eight years old. She interrupted, saying, "He can't hear you. He's deaf."

I anointed him and started praying. In about five minutes, he could hear everything I was saying. It was beautiful! He was healed. Thank you, Jesus!

It was a long but amazing weekend. Monday morning

came, and we had to go to work. On arriving at work, a war of words occurred about what God had done with the gas Friday. The result was a miracle of more paint being turned into gas and a man giving his heart to Jesus on the spot! Thank you, Jesus.

Later that day, management came to me and told me that I could pray for anyone who needed it. All they asked for was that we leave the line to do it.

A few days later they were bringing me sick managers to be prayed for. I remember one who they sent me to pray for told me the next stop was the hospital. This manager was a mess with severe diarrhea and nonstop bleeding. I prayed for her, and Jesus healed her. Again I say, "Thank you, Jesus."

I would like to go back to the miracle of the gas. I took a sample of the gas to test against the gas in my car. An eyedropper from my car burned for ten minutes on the ground. The eyedropper from God burned for two hours!

My Daughter's Account

It began when I found out when my dad was ill. My dad's eyelid began to look weird and grew a lump. My mom started to suggest to my dad that he needed to see the eye doctor and check out what his eye was doing. Dad refused and said he was fine. Mom continued to suggest the eye doctor, and finally, Dad agreed. They made an appointment and went to the eye doctor. The doctor looked at Dad's eye and looked confused. He left the room and came back and honestly admitted he didn't know what was going on. Nothing in his books explained what Dad's eye was doing. So he decided to send him to get checked out by a specialist. He went and got scanned. The doctors said he had a lesion in his eye that led into his brain.

My parents called a family meeting about my dad's current state. When I saw him, he acted fine, as if the big bump on his eye didn't cause him any issues. Dad explained what he saw, blurry and double vision. Mom said that he was going to a hospital to get an MRI scan. After we finished the family meeting, I walked around the house. I walked by my parents' room, and seeing Dad in his condition hurt my heart and made me worry. The next day, Mom and Dad went to the hospital, returning with something unbelievable.

Dad explained how he looked into the blue MRI light and saw Jesus for the first time. He told us how Jesus knew he was scared and that Dad was never going to admit it. It didn't seem like Dad was scared. He looked completely fine about what was happening. Dad also explained how Jesus was going to hold his right hand whenever he was scared during all this. I didn't know what to think. Was Dad going to be okay then? What was going to happen? Was this going to end soon?

The specialist decided to send Dad to a bigger hospital to get surgery. Coincidentally, most of our relatives lived in the area. We went to church first and then stayed home an extra day due to snow and icy roads. Then the next day was my dad's birthday, and we headed out on the long drive. We decided to stay with my grandma and grandpa. Mom and Dad decided to get Dad checked into the hospital and said goodbye to me and my siblings.

We sat around, waiting for any news about Dad. My siblings and I didn't really do anything. I was worried about Dad and wanted to call Mom to hear what the news was.

Mom finally got the news that the doctors were going to cut the top part of Dad's skull off and suck out the infection.

That would take up to eight hours, but the worst part was that Dad most likely wasn't going to live through it. If he didn't do the surgery, he wouldn't live through the night either. We didn't get to hear about that until later. About a few hours after the scheduled surgery, an intern came into Dad's hospital room and told him that the doctor had canceled, and they were sending him to a teaching hospital.

Right before the ambulance showed up, my grandma took my siblings and me to the hospital to say goodbye to Dad. We made it up to his room and said goodbye in the hallway outside his room. I cried like a baby as Dad told me he was going to fight no matter what to get back to us. We all hugged him and went back to Grandma's. Grandma then had to leave again to drive Mom to the teaching hospital since they wouldn't let her in the ambulance with Dad.

The next morning, Mom called; they gave us Dad's phone so we could talk to them. Once I heard Mom's voice, I silently cried. Mom told me Dad made it. He was sleeping, I think. They told us they were coming back soon and that they loved us. The phone call ended, and I was excited to see Mom and Dad again.

The next couple days were really boring. My siblings and I went to a trampoline gym place for kids. It was my cousin's birthday. Since this happened four years ago, the unimportant, boring days had no place in my memory. I only remember what happened when Mom and Dad came back. I wouldn't let go of Dad as he walked up the steps.

He was alive and well. I was so thankful. I am still thankful, and I have God and Jesus to thank for letting me keep my dad. I have seen so many miracles and healings since my dad was healed. I will never regret giving my heart to Jesus.

9

In Closing

Now it's time to bring this book to a close. I want you to know that God is standing there around each and every one of you. His arms are wide open, and he wants you to run into them. He loves you so much that he's willing to stand there and wait for you because he is such a gentleman. I love him so much, but you have to develop that love with him and become one of his workers. The harvest is plentiful, and the workers are few. I'm telling you we're all special in God's eyes. Every single one of us. Let him be the God of your life. Let Jesus be your Savior. He's coming, and he's coming soon.

This is simple. You don't have to go to college to do this. You don't need a ceremony for this. You don't need any of that. You can do this in the privacy of your own home. It's a simple prayer:

Jesus, I know I have hurt you, and I'm sorry. Forgive me of all my sins and become the Lord of my life. I worship you from this day forth. You are my King; you are my Messiah, I love you. Wash me in your blood; fill me with the Holy Spirit. In Jesus's mighty name, Amen.

If you say that and mean it, your life will change, and things will change for you.

I also ask that everyone sends feedback that you have given your heart to Jesus after reading this book. It is so important because God is going to bless this book. God has already blessed this book. There is power in this book. Thank you, Jesus.

Printed in the United States
by Baker & Taylor Publisher Services